# SOZO
# POWER

*CLAIMING YOUR NEW*
*SPIRITUAL BIRTHRIGHT IN CHRIST*

# HANK KUNNEMAN

One Voice Ministries
P.O. Box 390460
Omaha, NE 68139
855-777-7907
www.hankandbrenda.org

Sozo Power, Claiming Your New Spiritual Birthright
ISBN 978-0-9970645-8-2

# TABLE OF CONTENTS

**Chapter 1** | Blind from Birth / Claiming Your Rights

**Chapter 2** | Beyond Blessed

**Chapter 3** | It is Against the Law

**Chapter 4** | Forget Not Your Birthright

**Chapter 5** | Come to the Table

## CHAPTER ONE

## Blind from Birth / Claiming Your Rights

I will never forget the summer following my high school graduation when I knelt down and received Jesus into my heart in my basement bedroom of my parents' home. I have served the Lord for now over 35 years, but I didn't realize at that time what my salvation really provided for me. I was unaware, untaught, and blinded to my new spiritual birthright that came at the time of my salvation. You could say that I was blinded from my birth, both prophetically and naturally speaking. My eyes weren't opened until years later as to what Jesus really provides for those who call upon His name to be saved.

### Blind from Birth

When Jesus enters our lives, our eyes are opened and we understand His Word more clearly in what the Scripture calls "*so great a salvation*" (Hebrews 2:3). In John 9, we see a man Jesus healed who'd been born blind. His natural condition speaks to us prophetically of what is often our condition, spiritually speaking. We are blinded to the things Jesus intended for us to walk in as born-again believers. This can be because we only relate to things according to our natural birth, and we're completely unaware of what is fully available to us when we receive salvation. This was the case for me when I got saved.

Jesus passed by the man who'd been blind from his birth. "*And as Jesus passed by, he saw a man which was blind from his birth*" (John 9:1). Again, this verse prophetically speaks of what is often our condition, spiritually speaking, when we are first born again. Many times, we don't know what is spiritually and legally ours through Jesus' shed blood when we are first saved (born again). This results in us being like this man who was blind from birth; we can't fully see or understand what Jesus has provided for us.

## It is Time to See What is Yours as a Born-Again Believer

We need a recovery of sight to the blind, the sight Jesus declared the Holy Spirit had anointed Him to restore (see Luke 4:18). Once we understand what we *really* receive when we get saved, our eyes will no longer be blinded to our new spiritual birthright. This new spiritual birthright was established when Jesus came to earth to offer Himself as the only way of eternal salvation for man. In His birth, life, and death, is a full package of benefits for the believer in Christ.

*She will give birth to a Son, and you shall name Him Jesus (The Lord is salvation), for He will save His people from their sins"* (Matthew 1:21 AMP). This salvation that bore the definition of His name is also what He would provide by His death on the Cross, giving us what is called *soteria* or *sozo* rights, which encompasses salvation, healing, and deliverance (to name just a few) in every aspect of our lives.[1,2] When you are born again, you receive your new spiritual birthright. What is this? This is your inheritance, the spiritual rights you receive because of Jesus' sacrifice. It is freely given to sons and daughters of the Lord at the very moment we are born again!

*"And as members of the church of the Firstborn all our names have been legally registered as citizens of heaven! And we have come before God who judges all, and who lives among the spirits of the righteous who have been made perfect in his eyes"* (Hebrews 12:23 TPT).

*"Since we are receiving our rights to an unshakeable kingdom, we should be extremely thankful and offer God the purest worship that delights his heart as we lay down our lives in absolute surrender, filled with awe"* (Hebrews 12:28 TPT).

As members of the church of the Firstborn (Jesus being the first), upon our salvation we are entitled to our new spiritual birthright as part of His unshakable Kingdom. This makes us, as believers, joint heirs with Jesus and seated with Him in Heavenly places (see Ephesians 1). The same inheritance He received from His Father is also ours! You see, when Jesus entered into the Holy Place, the very Throne of God once and for all, He was carrying something in His hand. It was precious blood, not of bulls, sheep, goats, or calves used for sacrificing, but His own blood (see Hebrews 9:12). He then took His blood, and as the Scripture declares, put it upon the Mercy Seat of God, giving us grace, mercy, and help in the time of our need (see Hebrews 4:16). The blood was applied to the Mercy Seat. The Father then handed Jesus the scepter of Righteousness, which is the scepter of His Kingdom. The Father actually calls Jesus God (see Hebrews 1:8) and tells Him to sit at His right hand. In this transaction, Jesus is called *"the firstborn of many brethren"* and now entitles us to the same blessings of spiritual inheritance that He has received. We are made joint heirs and have a new spiritual birthright: the full sozo rights package! As a born-again believer, you are a joint heir to this promise, and it is time to take what is legally yours as an heir!

*"...and blessed with EVERY spiritual blessing in Christ! And if [we are] children, then heirs; heirs of God, and joint-heirs with Christ; if so be that we suffer with him, that we may be also glorified together"* (Romans 8:17).

This happens when you call upon the name of the Lord at the time of salvation! *"Whoever calls on the name of the Lord will be saved"* (Romans 10:13). You receive your sozo rights when you call upon the Lord to be saved.

You might be thinking, "This sounds great, but what exactly are sozo rights? In Romans 10:13, the word for "saved" is the Greek word *sozo* or *sodezo* and includes three contexts: salvation, healing, and deliverance.[2] All these elements are part of your new spiritual birthright! A more complete definition of *sozo* is: to save, to make whole or well, to deliver, heal, preserve, provide for, keep safe and sound, rescue from danger or destruction, rescue from injury or peril, to restore health, to heal.[2b] We must have our eyes opened to this marvelous truth of what is rightfully ours in Christ!

## We Must Know and Claim Our Sozo Rights!

Once we are born again, we must know what is included in our new spiritual birthright package. It is more than just salvation, forgiveness of sins, eternal life, and a mansion in Heaven. It is so much more! The problem is that many believers only receive or are aware of salvation (sozo) saving them from their sins. Sadly, this is where the power of sozo, or salvation, stops for most people. They often think the only thing they receive upon asking Jesus into their heart is salvation, not realizing the "full package" of sozo rights.

Again, it is important to understand what Jesus paid for completely, through His shed blood. We don't just receive forgiveness of sin and the promise of eternal life, but all the things that the word *sozo* means! We get so much more! Remember, those who call on the name of the Lord shall be saved, shall be made whole or well, shall be delivered, healed, preserved, provided for, kept safe and sound, rescued from danger or destruction, rescued from injury or peril, and shall be restored to health (see Luke 10:19).[2c]

## Avoiding the Nicodemus Mindset

If we want to truly receive our new spiritual birthright, we cannot be like Nicodemus, who understood the rights of Abraham, but didn't understand what could become his new spiritual birthright through Jesus the Messiah (see John 3). This is the situation with many Christians today who don't understand their new spiritual birthright or privileges. In order to live in the fullness of everything Jesus intends for us to have, we must stand for and claim our new birthright! This is why Jesus said we must be born again or we won't see the Kingdom.

 *"Jesus answered him, "I assure you and most solemnly say to you, unless a person is born again [reborn from above—spiritually transformed, renewed, sanctified], he cannot [ever] see and experience (emphasis mine) the kingdom of God"* (John 3:3 AMP).

Notice Jesus mentions two ways of "seeing." It is seeing and experiencing. He says we won't see Heaven, referring to our eternal life and eternal home, and we won't see or perceive Heaven's new spiritual birthright available to us when we give our lives to Jesus. This means we won't experience these spiritual blessings in Christ that are part of our new spiritual birthright, unless we perceive or understand them! To take it one step further, Jesus taught us to pray for the things He intends for us to have, by asking for our daily bread and praying His Kingdom will come to earth (see Luke 11).

Let's look at the story of Nicodemus to better understand the Nicodemus mindset:

*"There was a man named Nicodemus, a Jewish religious leader who was a Pharisee. After dark one evening, he came to speak with Jesus. "Rabbi," he said, "we all know that God has sent you to teach us. Your miraculous signs are evidence that God is with you." Jesus replied, "I tell you the truth, unless you are born again, you cannot see the Kingdom of God."*

*"What do you mean?" exclaimed Nicodemus. "How can an old man go back into his mother's womb and be born again?" Jesus replied, "I assure you, no one can enter the Kingdom of God without being born of water and the Spirit. Humans can reproduce only human life, but the Holy Spirit gives birth to spiritual life. So don't be surprised when I say, 'You must be born again.' The wind blows wherever it wants. Just as you can hear the wind but can't tell where it comes from or where it is going, so you can't explain how people are born of the Spirit."*

*"How are these things possible?" Nicodemus asked. Jesus replied, "You are a respected Jewish teacher, and yet you don't understand these things? I assure you, we tell you what we know and have seen, and yet you won't believe our testimony. But if you don't believe me when I tell you about earthly things, how can you possibly believe if I tell you about heavenly things?"* (John 3:1-12 NLT).

Again we see that Nicodemus, a Jewish man and leader, understood his rights under the Abrahamic covenant, but he didn't understand that he would have an opportunity to receive his new spiritual birthright through Jesus the Messiah by being born again. Many Christians don't know they have a new spiritual birthright, and don't know what it includes. We often hear people claim their natural inheritance, birthright, citizenship rights, ethnic heritage, or DNA family heritage, but we don't see the same drive to understand their new spiritual inheritance and birthright in Christ!

A birthright refers to that which one is entitled to by reason of birth, especially to the firstborn. We easily understand what a birthright is from a natural perspective, but if you are a born-again believer, you should truly stop to consider what this means from a spiritual perspective. When you were reborn to a new life in Christ, you received a birthright that entitles you to heavenly blessings. Remember, Jesus said, "you *must* be born again" to obtain your new spiritual birthright (see John 3).

In Genesis 25, we find the story of Jacob and Esau that teaches us the consequences of a wrong attitude, or lack of understanding toward one's Abrahamic birthright. The lessons in the story also apply to how we view our new spiritual birthright, because as believers, we are equally blessed under the covenant of Abraham (see Galatians 3:13-14).

Esau sold his natural birthright to his younger brother to fulfill his fleshly appetite for a bowl of stew. How does that relate to us? Let's think prophetically for a moment. When we are overly concerned about the natural world we live in or when we face a tough situation in our lives, we must not cheapen or ignore our spiritual birthright that Jesus fully paid for, at the expense of our flesh or out of ignorance.

Sometimes people sell out in the moment, like Esau did, without realizing what it will actually cost them. It is easy to go with whatever your fleshly appetite is, and our culture even encourages it; we are a compulsive, consumer-driven generation. As born-again believers, we have the Holy Spirit living within us and one of the fruits of the Spirit is self-control. This means we have the ability as new creations in Christ, to live by principle rather than compulsion; to not be led by our flesh but to be led by the Spirit; to think things through rather than giving in to what "feels good" in the moment. We must exercise our wills and stop to think when we make decisions. The Holy Spirit in us gives us the innate ability to choose to follow our principles instead of our flesh's compulsions.

In other words, we must always uphold the importance and understanding of sozo rights first and foremost, in every situation we face in life. It is critical that we don't ever cheapen our birthright!

After all, Scripture says we perish for a lack of knowledge (see Hosea 4:6). We are settling for less, like Esau, when we lack full knowledge, understanding, or honor towards what we received upon salvation. We've received our *sozo*, (our new spiritual birthright) and that should never be taken lightly, the way Esau treated his birthright. These are our spiritual blessings, our new birthright package, all wrapped up in the Greek word *sozo*!

## ENDNOTES

1. James Strong, The New Strong's Exhaustive Concordance of the Bible (Nashville, TN:  Thomas Nelson, 1991), Greek #4991.

2. Ibid., Greek #4982.

## CHAPTER TWO

### Beyond Blessed

Have you ever heard someone say that they are "beyond blessed?" If we truly understand what we received at the time of our salvation, we'd call ourselves "beyond blessed" too! We are beyond blessed because we receive more than just eternity in heaven and the forgiveness of sins. The Greek word for salvation in Romans 10:13 is *sozo* and it is the glorious full-benefits package of being a joint heir with Jesus.1 As we mentioned in the previous chapter, our sozo rights become ours when we call upon the Lord to be saved (see Romans 10:13). *Sozo* is a small word with a big meaning; it tells us that when we are born again, we actually receive salvation, wholeness, wellness, deliverance, healing, health, preservation, protection, rescue, and provision![1b]

Hebrews 2:3 tells us that we have "such a great salvation." Here, salvation is the word *soteria* which has its origin in *sozo*, as we described earlier.[2] It is translated as "salvation," which means to deliver, health, salvation, and save. The reason there is power in our salvation is because *sozo / soteria* is made available to us (see Romans 1:16, 17). It is not hard to see or say that we are beyond blessed, because we really are! We see this reality in Ephesians 1:3: *"blessed be our God and Father of our Lord Jesus Christ, who hath blessed us (emphasis mine) with all spiritual blessings in Heavenly places in Christ."*

Did you see it? We are beyond blessed because God has already blessed us, meaning, it's past tense; it has already taken place! He has blessed those who have received Jesus Christ in their lives with *all* spiritual blessings, available upon salvation and anytime needed. These blessings are our covenant rights in Him and what we're calling *sozo* rights. We are beyond blessed because He is the God who has done and will always do, exceedingly, abundantly, beyond all that we ask or think (see Ephesians 3:20)! It is His nature to do us good, and what has been provided in our salvation "benefits package" is far beyond what we've asked or thought!

It is important to know that the word "blessing" in Ephesians 1:3 is a translation of the Greek word *eulogeo* and it's where we get the word "eulogy."[3] It literally means "to speak well of." This means God has spoken good things about us, or pronounced good things, for our benefit. We see this also in the creation with Adam and Eve. One of the first things God does is bless them, meaning also "to pronounce or speak blessings" (see Genesis 1:28).4 It is vital that we do the same in speaking blessings over our lives, especially the blessings that come with our sozo rights. We will talk more about this in Chapter Four.

## How to Receive What is Ours

Let's continue to look at our new spiritual birthright, or what we call our sozo rights benefits package. What a glorious salvation we have! Again, once we call on the name of the Lord to be saved, we receive forgiveness for our sins, but we also receive eternal life in Christ Jesus and so much more! So how do we receive these benefits?

It starts by believing in our hearts that God raised Jesus from the dead, and confessing with our mouth that He is Lord, calling upon Him to be saved.

*"That if thou shalt confess with thy mouth the Lord Jesus, and shalt believe in thine heart that God hath raised him from the dead, thou shalt be saved. For with the heart man believeth unto righteousness; and with the mouth confession is made unto salvation"* (Romans 10:9-10).

This is key in actually *activating* our sozo rights, rather than just having a vague understanding of their existence. It comes as we fully understand and believe that when the Father raised His Son Jesus from the dead, these rights were given to Him and also to us. We then confess them or speak them and they are activated to operate in our lives, bringing all their benefits! This is one of the meanings of calling upon the name of the Lord to be saved. If we are not fully aware of or receiving what has already been made available to us, we may need to re-examine our beliefs. The problem often lies in thinking this is a one-time experience, coming only at the time of salvation. However, this right we have to call upon the Lord to be saved is both a one-time experience *and* also an as-often-as-we-need experience! Any day, any minute, any second, we can call upon the Lord to be saved. Again, this is not just a one-time event; we can claim our covenant, sozo rights, *anytime*!

**Stand on Your Feet**

Now that we understand what is fully ours, we must take care to not have a beggar's attitude about our God-given sozo rights. Think of this: when withdrawing money from our savings account at the bank, we don't approach the teller begging and pleading for them to give us our money. No! We fully expect them to give to us what is rightfully and legally ours. In the same way, we don't need to beg God, cry, or plead with Him when it comes to our sozo rights. After all, they are *fully* ours through what Jesus paid for and deposited in Heaven. Remember, He put His own blood that He carried into the Holy Place, onto the Mercy Seat and sat down at the right hand of His Father, making you a joint heir to all He paid for. No begging needed!

I want to share with you a story from Acts, chapter three, of a man born physically lame and daily begging for handouts. This must not become our habit concerning our understanding or approach to our new spiritual birthright in Christ. We must remember our spiritual birthright is not a beggar's handout, because in Christ we are no longer beggars. Our birthright is our inheritance as sons and daughters of God. It belongs to us because of what Jesus legally provided. Yes, it was freely handed to us by God, but it's not something we must beg Him to give us; it is joyfully given to us as children who have full rights to what the Father has provided!

If we approach our birthright as poor sinners or unworthy, underserving servants, we will adopt a begging and spiritually-lame mindset. Living from this place will cause us not to stand on our feet in all the promises God has provided for us. Let's look at the story:

*Now Peter and John went up together into the temple at the hour of prayer, being the ninth hour. And a certain man lame from his mother's womb was carried, whom they laid daily at the gate of the temple which is called Beautiful, to ask alms of them that entered into the temple; Who seeing Peter and John about to go into the temple asked an alms. And Peter, fastening his eyes upon him with John, said, "Look on us." And he gave heed unto them, expecting to receive something of them. Then Peter said, "Silver and gold have I none; but such as I have give I thee: In the name of Jesus Christ of Nazareth rise up and walk." And he took him by the right hand, and lifted him up: and immediately his feet and ankle bones received strength. And he leaping up stood, and walked, and entered with them into the temple, walking, and leaping, and praising God. And all the people saw him walking and praising God* (Acts 3:1-8).

The man had laid lame at the Gate Beautiful from the time of his birth. When Peter showed up, he gave what he had spiritually to the man by speaking the true inheritance in Christ and instructing him to rise up and walk. Really, Peter was saying, "receive what I have received from Jesus, that I'm giving to you. It's yours!" As Peter declared to the lame man the sozo rights that Peter himself had received, the man stood up and walked! More than that, he was seen *"...leaping, and praising God"* (Acts 3:8).

**Dance, Leap, and Praise in Your Rights!**

In the same way, once we receive what is ours and fully understand it, this needs to be our posture and our expression regarding what Jesus provided for us. This man wasn't begging or carrying on in the same condition he had lived every day. He was standing in his new birthright, healed, leaping, and dancing in the temple. This is crucial for living in our sozo rights: we must be thankful and celebrate what is *already* ours!

Remember, you are not a beggar; you have a completely new birthright that you need to receive! The birthright will change the way you live your life, just like it changed this beggar's life. He started off lame and the next thing you know, he was jumping all over the place and praising God! It's time to start making withdrawals from your heavenly account. Take what is already yours!

## Such as I Have, I Give You

Let's look at the story from a slightly different angle for a minute. Let's look at Peter. Peter, the hot-headed fisherman. Peter, the one who was quick on impulse and slow on thinking. Peter, the one who denied Christ. He must have felt like he'd thrown his whole life away when he denied Jesus. I'm sure he thought Jesus would never have any use for him. But in John 21, Jesus reassured Peter that he still had a future with Him (see v. 18-19). Though Peter had denied Him, he would eventually give up his own life for Jesus. The first few chapters of Acts show Peter beginning to walk in his sozo rights. By the time he gets to the lame man at the Gate Beautiful, he demonstrates the truth of inheritance with the man, and it changes his life forever!

Maybe you feel like you've blown it too many times, or you feel like Jesus wouldn't ever want to use you. Those are lies. In the same way He saw Peter's future, He sees yours. And He is excited! Your inheritance is still inside you, just like Peter's was. See, even though Peter messed up, his sozo rights never changed. No matter how you've messed up, you can't change the fact that you are *beyond blessed* and have a wonderful inheritance! Peter could demonstrate sozo power to the lame man, because Peter himself understood what he carried.

I want to encourage you to see yourself as both characters in this story.  See yourself as the lame man and know that you can rise up and walk. And see yourself as Peter, realizing that you still have a great hope, a great future, and great sozo power inside you! Once you're confident in declaring it over yourself, you can declare sozo power over others. Now stand on your feet and don't ignore your great salvation. Fully receive today the rights and privileges of your birthright package because you are beyond blessed!

## ENDNOTES

1. James Strong, The New Strong's Exhaustive Concordance of the Bible (Nashville, TN:  Thomas Nelson, 1991), Greek #4982.

2. Ibid., Greek #4991.

3. Ibid., Greek #2127.

4. Ibid., Hebrew #1288.

## CHAPTER THREE

### It Is Against the Law

The entire universe is governed by laws. There are laws of nature like the law of gravity, the law of attraction, and other laws of physics. Under the laws of nature, if we do something like drop a glass full of water, it will hit the ground and break. The law of gravity is at work and we are under that law in the natural world. We are also governed by laws in our society. If we break these laws, we go before the judge to face our sentence (or punishment) for what we've done.

If a person commits a felony, their sentence could be prison time. If someone commits a misdemeanor, they will probably be given a fine and sent on their way, depending on the crime involved. No matter what the consequences are, the fact is, we are subject to laws.

Before we accepted Christ, we *were* under the law of sin and death. But at the moment of our salvation, we are set free from that law, and are to then be governed by the law of the

Spirit of Life in Christ Jesus as we grow in our understanding of the power of our salvation.

God's intention for us is wholeness, sozo, and it has *already* been provided to us, given at the time we are born again. Our mindset needs to be renewed, that we are not trying to become free from sin. The truth is, we are *already* free from sin and we've *already* been delivered from things associated with sin and death, like sickness and disease. *"...because through Christ Jesus the law of the Spirit who gives life has set you free (emphasis mine) from the law of sin and death"* (Romans 8:2).

It is important to note that sickness in any form is a result of the curse, or the law of sin and death. Being set free from this law includes being set free from physical and emotional ailments of every kind. This is the abundant life that Jesus intends for us to enjoy and is part of working out our salvation to a life of complete victory (see Philippians 2: 12-13)!

Never settle for less, because Jesus said, *"The thief cometh not, but for to steal, and to kill, and to destroy; I am come that they might have life, and that they might have it more abundantly"* (John 10:10).

As believers, therefore, we need to understand that it is illegal for sickness and that which is connected to the law of sin and death, to reign in our lives or bodies. Jesus promised us life and life more abundantly, which is to live healthy and whole. Your new birthright is an abundant, blessed life!

God has promised *"...he has restored your health and healed you of every affliction"* and *"promised to meet your every need according to His riches and glory in Christ Jesus"* (Jeremiah

30:17; Philippians 4:19).

Are you starting to see what your legal new birthright looks like? It's every disease healed, every need met, according to His abundant blessing. Oh, what a Savior we have!

The first Passover is another powerful demonstration of our legal New Covenant birthright. In the Passover, the birthright was enforced through applying the lamb's blood as protection over His people. This was a legal transaction for the children of Israel that would bring protection and blood rights, if they would obey His word. It is a tremendously vivid picture of the Cross, as they applied the blood to the top and sides of the doorposts forming the shape of a cross. In the same way, Jesus provided His own blood on the Cross as our legal protection and provision. We can now apply His blood to our lives through understanding and speaking our sozo rights!

Remember, we have the full package! Jesus' death on the Cross provided our righteousness, our perfection, and our *legal* citizenship in heaven! We are no longer under the law of sin and death. Instead, we've been given life and life more abundantly; this is sozo!

We are citizens of heaven, with our spiritual new birthright. *"And as members of the underline{church of the Firstborn} (emphasis mine) all our names have been underline{legally registered} as citizens of heaven (emphasis mine)! And we have come before God who judges all, and who lives among the spirits of the righteous who have been made perfect in his eyes"* (Hebrews 12:23 TPT)!

We can see from this verse that the sacrificial blood of Jesus gave us blood rights, which are citizenship rights.  Romans 8:29 also says that Jesus is the "firstborn" of many brethren.

You could say He was the first rightful citizen of the Kingdom of God. He was the first legal "blood-born" citizen and when we receive His blood, we legally become rightful citizens, too. In the same way that we have certain rights in the nation where we're born on earth, we have legal rights as a citizen of heaven!

For this reason, our salvation is called "so great a salvation," and it is truly a great gift exchange (see Hebrews 2:3)! We received the right to heavenly citizenship the moment we received Jesus' sacrifice by faith. We legally gave up our former citizenship in darkness and have now been legally translated to citizenship in a new Kingdom (see Colossians 1:13). We exchanged our former citizenship for a new one!

This exchange can be likened to when the wise men came to Jesus and opened their hearts, their treasures. In return, they received the revelation of Jesus as Messiah and all that He is in their worship.

When we open our hearts and present them to the Lord, He in return, welcomes us into the family, giving us our full inheritance of sonship. The great exchange is our life given to Him and in return, His life, health, blessings, provision, and deliverance (to name just a few) are given to us as members of the heavenly family.

We see another example of this great exchange in His death as described in Isaiah 53. Let's look a little closer at these wonderful verses:

*"He is despised and rejected of men; a man of sorrows, and acquainted with grief: and we hid as it were our faces from him; he was despised, and we esteemed him not. Surely he*

*hath borne our grief (SICKNESS), and carried our sorrows (PAINS): yet we did esteem him stricken, smitten of God, and afflicted. But he was wounded for our transgressions, he was bruised for our iniquities: the chastisement of our peace was upon him; and with his stripes we are healed. All we like sheep have gone astray; we have turned every one to his own way; and the Lord hath laid on him the iniquity of us all. He was oppressed, and he was afflicted, yet he opened not his mouth: he is brought as a lamb to the slaughter, and as a sheep before her shearers is dumb, so he openeth not his mouth"* (Isaiah 53:3-7).

This gift exchange is Jesus offering His life, taking our sins, sicknesses, diseases, pains, and in exchange, providing our healing and so much more.

What Jesus provided here is what we call our sozo rights package. It's legally ours! As a heavenly citizen, you have a legal right to be healed today! It was not just our spiritual or emotional healing, but also our physical healing. In Him and through His shed blood, we have legal right to every aspect of healing: physical, emotional, and spiritual.

In Matthew 8:16-17, Matthew quotes Isaiah 53:4 this way: *"When the even was come, they brought unto him many that were possessed with devils: and he cast out the spirits with his word, and healed all that were sick: That it might be fulfilled which was spoken by Esaias [Isaiah] the prophet, saying, Himself took our infirmities, and bare our sicknesses."*

The emphasis is on physical healing in this verse. Matthew, under the inspiration of the Holy Spirit, substituted the words "infirmities" and "sicknesses" for Isaiah's words "griefs" and "sorrows" in Isaiah 53. We see the Lord's intent to bless us in this wonderful gift exchange.

His desire to bless us is also evident when we see Jesus asking the question, "What do you want Me to do for you?" Throughout the Gospels, Jesus often asks this question as He encounters people who need a touch from Him. He asks them to tell Him what they need. He wants them to verbalize what they need. He wants the same from us today. Jesus loves to hear us express our hearts to Him. Of course, He already knows what we need, but there's something about our telling Him our need that moves His heart. I believe He loves it when we get a revelation of who He is and what He's done for us!

Let me ask you: what do you need the Lord to do for you? Do you need physical healing? Jesus is the same yesterday, today, and forever. His shed blood has provided everything you need. Ask Him, and you will receive the revelation of the law of the Spirit of Life in Christ Jesus, the law that has set you free from sin and death!

Think of your sozo rights package as a literal package, one that Jesus has given to you. Yes, you have it; now it's time to open this beautiful package and start enjoying what's inside: life abundantly, healing in every way you need it, provision, protection, wholeness. Whatever you need, you've got it! Remember, we're not trying to *become* something different or new; we've *already* been made new because a law has been established. We are legal citizens with legal rights! We're not trying to get something; we're learning to walk in the reality of what we've already received!

## Are and Already Were

I want to draw your attention to two important words in Scripture regarding healing: "are" and "were." These may seem to contradict each other, but they actually go hand in hand. In Isaiah 53:5, we are told that we *are* healed. In 1 Peter 2:24, we are told that we *were* healed.

*"But He was wounded for our transgressions; He was bruised for our iniquities. The chastisement of our peace was upon Him, and with His stripes <u>we are healed</u> (emphasis mine)"* (Isaiah 53:5).

*"Who his own self bare our sins in his own body on the tree, that we, being dead to sins, should live unto righteousness: by whose stripes <u>ye were healed</u> (emphasis mine)"* (1 Peter 2:24).

This may sound strange, but as part of our salvation (sozo rights), we *are already healed, already provided for, already delivered*. You might be thinking, "but I've got a doctor's report to prove I don't have healing," or "I have an unexpected bill that proves I don't have blessing." Regardless of what the natural facts are, the truth is that God has already given you exactly what you need. Natural facts are visible and we do not deny those, but the doctor's report of sickness and your stack of paper bills are not under the law of the Spirit of Life in Christ Jesus. They are natural facts, and therefore, under the law of sin and death. You can look at the natural facts and submit them to the truth that you have been set free from that law!

2 Peter 1:3 says, *"According as his divine power <u>hath given unto us</u> (emphasis mine) all things that <u>pertain unto life and godliness</u> (emphasis mine), through the knowledge of him that hath called us to glory and virtue."*

We have been given all things that pertain to life and godliness. This is the truth! It is critical that we receive this knowledge of what Jesus provided in our sozo new birthright package. If we are not living in this knowledge, we are believing a lie and that lie will give the enemy access to harass us and keep us in physical sickness, financial or physical lack, and emotional distress.

Why is this? The Scripture tells us we are lacking knowledge. *"My people are destroyed for a lack of knowledge"* (Hosea 4:6).

You see, the enemy will do everything he can to keep us from believing the truth. He may try to distract us by making the facts seem larger than the truth. It's important to renew our minds (see Romans 12:2) so that focusing on the truth (knowledge of our legal rights) becomes our habit, instead of focusing on the circumstances we are facing in the natural realm. *Set your mind on the things above, not on the things that are on earth; for you died, and your life is hidden with Christ in God* (Col. 3:2-3).

Whatever you are facing, remember God has provided everything you need through Jesus and His shed blood. Healing is for *all* at *all* times! It is always His will for you to be healed, every time, of every affliction, because He has purchased it and provided it through His blood!

The Lord wants to bless you and meet your needs. He demonstrates this as people came to Jesus and He healed them *all*!

*"When evening had come, they brought to Him many who were demon-possessed. And He cast out the spirits with a word and healed all who were sick"* (Matthew 8:16).

*"But when Jesus knew it, He withdrew from there. And great multitudes followed Him, and He healed them all"* (Matthew 12:15).

*"And the whole multitude sought to touch Him, for power went out from Him and healed them all"* (Luke 6:19).

*"But when the multitudes knew it, they followed Him; and He received them and spoke to them about the kingdom of God and healed those who had need of healing"* (Luke 9:11).

*"...how God anointed Jesus of Nazareth with the Holy Spirit and with power, who went about doing good and healing all who were oppressed by the devil, for God was with Him"* (Acts 10:38).

The Greek word for "all" used in the original text is pas and it occurs more than one thousand times in the Bible.[1] It means "all, the whole/entire, every kind of." There was no sick person that went to Jesus in faith that was not healed of whatever disease or disability they had. There is no verse in the Bible that says that it was not our heavenly Father's will for them all to be healed.

**But...**

We see that whenever people came to Him, Jesus *healed them all*, except in a case where it mentions that He couldn't. It doesn't say He *wouldn't*! Why would Jesus *not* be able to heal someone? Scripture tells us it was because of *their* unbelief / unwillingness, not His!

*"And he went out from thence, and came into his own country; and his disciples follow him. And when the sabbath day was come, he began to teach in the synagogue: and many*

*hearing him were astonished, saying, From whence hath this man these things? and what wisdom is this which is given unto him, that even such mighty works are wrought by his hands? Is not this the carpenter, the son of Mary, the brother of James, and Joses, and of Juda, and Simon? and are not his sisters here with us? And they were offended at him. But Jesus, said unto them, A prophet is not without honour, but in his own country, and among his own kin, and in his own house. And he could there do no mighty work, save that he laid his hands upon a few sick folk, and healed them. And he marvelled because of their unbelief (emphasis mine)"* (Mark 6:1-6).

Again, Jesus did His part on the Cross showing He was willing by providing our salvation, our spiritual new birthright: sozo! Let's believe so that we can receive!

## Experience or Word?

You may be thinking, "Pastor Hank, I know someone who believed and prayed, and they didn't get healed, or they prayed for something and nothing happened. What do you do with situations like that?" Well, we must be careful not to base the Word of God, Jesus' shed blood, and our lack of visible blessings, healing, or provision, on our experiences! When we do this, we are typically focusing on the natural world around us, our circumstances, and everything we see with our physical eyes. Instead, settle it in your heart that it is the will of God for you to be healed and blessed! Remember, we are under the Spirit of Life in Christ Jesus. We must be careful or we will treat the blood of Jesus with contempt and false accusations through negativity and unbelief. Jesus' shed blood was *not* shed in vain. It provided us with everything we need! Again, settle it in your heart that it is the will of God for you to be healed and blessed!

We know that not everyone gets healed; not even all those who desire healing receive it. It is not because it hasn't been made available through Jesus' shed blood. To deal with this dilemma, the doctrine that it's not always God's will to heal has arisen. That's convenient. That makes it God's fault and not ours, if things don't go right. However, that is not what the Word of God teaches. The fountain of His blood is flowing, the bread has been provided (see Zechariah 13:1; Matthew 6:11). Jesus Himself taught us to pray, *"Give us this day our daily bread"* (Matthew 6:11). Our daily bread includes healing, provision, or whatever we need. Depending on the day, we might need a slice, or we may need the whole loaf! The point is, we can access what we need whenever we need it. Again, Jesus healed all, but not all were healed. As we mentioned, this was because of unbelief. Don't let any circumstance or any person talk you out of your right to be healed!

## What Color is That Wall?

If the wall you are looking at is red, don't let anyone tell you that it's blue. In other words, if Jesus has *already* healed you through His blood, then don't let anyone talk you out of it or convince you otherwise. Focusing on His Word, His promises, rather than on your experiences, will seal His truth in your heart.

Most Christians believe that God *can* do anything, but many of them don't believe He *has done* very much. In Genesis 17:1-2, God calls himself *El Shaddai,* "God Almighty," meaning "the God of more-than-enough."[2] He has always been and will always be, more than enough for us! We must be wise to not live in a constant state of trying to get God to do something. This leads to begging God to move or asking Him to give what He's already provided. The problem with this is that we're trying to get something from God, not realizing we already have it.

There is always more going on than what we see with our natural eyes. The key is to understand that God is spirit and moves in the spirit realm (see John 4:24). Whether or not we see a physical manifestation of what He has done in the spiritual realm is dependent upon what we believe and how we act, not on what He has done. He's already healed us (see 1 Peter 2:24).

God loves faith. In fact, without it, it is impossible to please Him (see Hebrews 11:6). A study of the Gospels will quickly reveal Jesus telling people over and over, *"your faith has made you well"* (Mark 5:34) or *"be it done according to your faith"* (Matthew 9:29). Faith is important to Him. It moves Him. And when we don't see and still believe, He calls us blessed (see John 20:29)!

Healing has already been provided. Financial prosperity has already been provided. Joy, peace, a better quality of life, and everything you will ever need emotionally have already been provided. We should not ever doubt something that we already have through Jesus' shed blood!

## Do You Know What You Have?

Let's say I give my wallet to someone, telling them it is now theirs and they can have everything inside. What would happen if they stood there holding it and asked me for my wallet? I would probably just look at them and say, "I already gave it to you, and everything inside!"

Many Christians, when they pray, act like they are still waiting for God to give them "the wallet," or their sozo rights package. He's already given it to us, with everything we need inside! Ephesians 1 tells us this again: *"Blessed be the God and Father of our Lord Jesus Christ, who hath [past tense] blessed us with all spiritual blessings in heavenly places in Christ"* (v.3).

We see a type of this example with the wallet, of knowing what's already ours, in the story of the Prodigal Son. This powerful story gives us two angles on not living in the fullness of what we've been given.

The prodigal son got the full package that he didn't deserve. He had been impatient, demanded his inheritance, and very much took it for granted. But the father received him with open arms when he came home. In fact, the father lavished his son with affection, not because of anything he did, but simply because he was his son!

And the elder brother got angry. Right? He didn't realize the Father had given him full rights to everything he owned as well. His father reminded him, "everything I have is yours!" (see Luke 15:31). The disconnection was the same one we have from our Heavenly Father: he didn't know it was available to him, or that his father wanted him to have it!

*"Meanwhile, the older son was in the field. When he came near the house, he heard music and dancing. So he called one of the servants and asked him what was going on. 'Your brother has come,' he replied, 'and your father has killed the fattened calf because he has him back safe and sound.'" The older brother became angry and refused to go in. So his father went out and pleaded with him. But he answered his father, 'Look! All these years I've been slaving for you and never disobeyed your orders. Yet you never gave me even a young goat so I*

*could celebrate with my friends. But when this son of yours
who has squandered your property with prostitutes comes
home, you kill the fattened calf for him!' "'My son,' the father
said, 'you are always with me, and everything I have is yours.
But we had to celebrate and be glad, because this brother of
yours was dead and is alive again; he was lost and is found'"*
(Luke 15:25-32).

**Argue Your Case!**

As displayed in what we just read with the prodigal son's
elder brother, you must take what is already yours. If sickness,
disease, pain, sorrow, depression, or lack (to name a few) are
attacking you, rise up and argue your case on the basis of
your legal right through the Blood of Jesus! Declare that these
things are against the law of the Spirit of Life in Christ. Speak to
your situation, "I am no longer under this law of sin and death,
sickness, disease, depression (or whatever you're experiencing).
I am under the Law of the Spirit of Life in Christ Jesus!"

If someone broke into your home to attack you and to take
what is not theirs, you would do everything in your power to
stop them. This must be your attitude when it comes to your
life!

Remember, as believers "passed over" by the sentence of death
and set free from the law of sin and death, we are *fully entitled*
to abundant life! It is our family right, our new birthright, our
blood-bought right, our sozo package right! Anything contrary
to our new birthright is illegal, because we are under the law
of the Spirit of Life, and life abundantly (see Romans 8:2; John
10:10). It is true, but we have to believe it, confess it, and walk in
it day by day!

You see, every good thing is already in you in Christ. God has already provided all that we need through Jesus' death on the Cross. The last few words Jesus spoke on the Cross were, *"It is finished,"* and this settles our case (John 19:30). You now have access to your new spiritual birthright, your new life in Christ Jesus. Make the choice to live under the new spiritual law of Life in Christ. Don't be afraid to tell the enemy that what he is doing to rob you is AGAINST THE LAW!

## ENDNOTES

1. James Strong, The New Strong's Exhaustive Concordance of the Bible (Nashville, TN: Thomas Nelson, 1991), Greek #3956.

2. Ibid., Hebrew #7706.

## CHAPTER FOUR

### Forget Not Your Birthright

In Psalm 103, David instructs us to *"bless the Lord... and forget not all His benefits..."*. Notice, not just SOME of His benefits, but ALL! We are too often content to settle for *some* when God wants us to experience *all*! We've talked about the benefits of our new birthright, our wonderful gift of sozo the Lord has provided for us. We must also remember, however, that we have a part to play in receiving what He's provided. Our part is to "bless the Lord...and forget not all His benefits."

What does this look like? We know we've been handed "the wallet," but we must be able to access and use what's inside: our healing, our freedom, our rescue, our abundant provision. Our part is remembering, acknowledging, and being thankful. Acknowledging what God has done for us allows us to see more of His goodness in our lives every day. Thankfulness changes our focus from our need to His provision. Remember the ten lepers who were healed? Only one returned to give Jesus thanks. That one man has a beautiful testimony. I wonder about the other nine.

*Jesus traveled on toward Jerusalem and passed through the border region between Samaria and Galilee. As he entered one village, ten men approached him, but they kept their distance, for they were lepers. They shouted to him, "Mighty Lord, our wonderful Master! Won't you have mercy on us and heal us?" When Jesus stopped to look at them, he spoke these words: "Go to be examined by the Jewish priests." They set off, and they were healed while walking along the way. One of them, a foreigner from Samaria, when he discovered that he was completely healed, turned back to find Jesus, shouting out joyous praises and glorifying God. When he found Jesus, he fell down at his feet and thanked him over and over, saying to him, "You are the Messiah." This man was a Samaritan. "So where are the other nine?" Jesus asked. "Weren't there ten who were healed? They all refused to return to give thanks and give glory to God except you, a foreigner from Samaria?" Then Jesus said to the healed man lying at his feet, "Arise and go. It was your faith that brought you salvation and healing"* (Luke 17:11-19).

Thankfulness starts with realizing what we've received. Ten lepers' lives were changed that day but nine of them didn't even say "thank you." It is also interesting that the man who returned was a foreigner; he wasn't familiar with Jesus, as perhaps the other nine had been, who the Bible never mentions were foreigners. In our "grab-and-go" culture, we can be tempted to rush away from the Lord, without thanking Him for what He's done for us. Let's never become so familiar with the Lord that we do this. The bottom line is not healing or restoration, but our relationship with Him! Thankfulness is an integral part of relationship and brings a higher level of blessings, as we see with this one leper who returned to give thanks. He wasn't just healed; he was made whole.

*Bless the Lord, O my soul: and all that is within me, bless his holy name. Bless the Lord, O my soul, and forget not all his benefits: Who forgiveth all thine iniquities; who healeth all thy diseases; Who redeemeth thy life from destruction; who crowneth thee with lovingkindness and tender mercies; Who satisfieth thy mouth with good things; so that thy youth is renewed like the eagle's. The Lord executes righteousness and justice for all who are oppressed. He made known His ways to Moses, His acts to the children of Israel* (Psalm 103:1-7).

These are our new spiritual birthrights that must not be forgotten! We can see from these verses that God has provided wonderful benefits for us as His children. But *before* David lists the promises, he says "bless the Lord, O my soul." He is commanding his soul to bless the Lord. The word "bless" in Hebrew is *barak*, and it means to praise or to kneel down.1 Do you see that? David is making an intentional choice to position his soul in thankfulness, just like the leper who returned to thank Jesus.

These promises are incredible! God has done what no one else can do for us! He's done what we can't do for ourselves. How can we be anything less than thankful? Well, truthfully, we *can* be less than thankful. We can be one of those nine lepers who didn't return to thank Jesus. We don't like to see ourselves that way, but if we're honest, we don't always run to thank Him. Sometimes we do take things for granted and sometimes we feel like we've made too many mistakes. Don't let mistakes or regret keep you from receiving what the Lord has provided. Did you notice the first part of your benefits package started with forgiveness from all iniquity (see Psalm 103:3)? In other words, He has forgiven your sin first and foremost so you can fully receive what He has provided for you; your receiving is not based on your mistakes or feelings of unworthiness.

You may think thankfulness is a natural response, but it is actually a choice. It is an act of our will. In the same way the foreigner healed of leprosy returned to thank Jesus, in the same way David commanded his soul to bless the Lord, we must take charge of our will and make the choice to praise God and be thankful. Our thankfulness will produce a response / a physical action. Thankfulness looks like something; it has a recognizable expression. It is always appropriate to say thank you when you receive something good! As we meditate on His Word and allow truth to fill our minds, it helps our will line up with His, and thankfulness becomes the easy choice. Read that again; don't rush ahead. We *meditate* on His Word. We think on it. We rehearse it over and over in our minds. We really take time to think about it. We let the truth change us.

There is a huge key here to living in the fullness of our birthright. *"Forget not all His benefits."* We must remember what God has done! We are transformed by the renewing of our minds (see Romans 12). Meditating on the Scripture, especially on what God has provided, on who we are as His children, and on the qualities of abundant life that Jesus has given, will change our focus. Our thoughts shape our lives. As we meditate on His Word, the facts of that doctor's report get replaced with the truth of, *"by His stripes I am healed"* (Isaiah 53:5). The feelings of guilt are replaced with confidence in the God who *"forgives all our sins"* (Psalm 103:3). We can't be casual about this. Changing the way we think will change our lives. It is how we open the wallet and use the sozo rights inside! God has given us *everything* we need. We have a new birthright, and the benefits are too many to count! But we cannot ignore our part. Let's position ourselves in thankfulness and "forget not all His benefits!"

## Let the Redeemed of the Lord Say So

In the same way meditation is important, it's just as important that we confess what the Lord has done for us. This is one way we remember His benefits. Psalm 107:2 says *"Let the redeemed of the Lord say so..."*. Why? because you have been redeemed from the hand of the enemy; you have a new birthright! To elaborate a little more: you've been set free from the law of sin and death. You've been made new. You are healed. You are rescued. You are whole. You are provided for abundantly. You are loved extravagantly. You are in Christ, fully alive. You are an heir of sozo rights!

*Oh, give thanks to the Lord, for He is good! For His mercy endures forever. Let the redeemed of the Lord say so, Whom He has redeemed from the hand of the enemy* (Psalm 107:1-2).

Think about it, all throughout Scripture we see God doing the very thing our sozo rights provide. He protected and rescued the children of Israel from Pharaoh, and He drowned Pharoah's army in the Red Sea. When Shadrach, Meshach, and Abednego were thrown into the fire, He was the "fourth man" walking around with them. He shut the lions' mouths so Daniel was able to spend the night with them and come out without a scratch. He delivered those bound by evil spirits; He set them free with a word, a touch, or an angelic visitation. He healed countless people, especially through the ministry of Jesus and the apostles. God's protection and rescue of His people is visible throughout history and all the way into today. We all have stories of how God has intervened on our behalf. We've all seen evidence of our sozo rights package in action!

With our mouths we make our confessions unto salvation. And with our mouths we remind God and the enemy of our full rights in Christ Jesus. Our words matter. Speaking is meditating out loud. When we "say so," remembering what God has done for us in the past or confessing our new sozo rights package benefits, we activate the Word on our behalf. *Faith comes by hearing, and hearing by the Word of God* (Romans 10:17).

*That if thou shalt confess with thy mouth the Lord Jesus, and shalt believe in thine heart that God hath raised him from the dead, thou shalt be saved. For with the heart man believeth unto righteousness; and with the mouth confession is made unto salvation* (Romans 10:9-10).

The more we speak, the more our faith grows. Speaking your sozo rights over yourself is a wonderful way to activate your faith. If you have a hard time seeing God's faithfulness in your life, read Scripture out loud. Declare the testimonies in Psalms 103 and 107, and know that He is the same yesterday, today, and forever! The same God who rescued the children of Israel is on your side! He made known His ways to Moses, His acts to the children of Israel (Psalm 103:7).

**Our Deliverer**

He was, is, and always will be, our Rescuer and Redeemer. We have full access to His protection and provision in our new benefits package! The Hebrew boys were thrown into the fire because they stood their ground and refused to worship idols (see Daniel 3:18). They knew the God they served, and they were *still thrown into the fire*. It's easy to read about their rescue, now that we know the end of the story. But they didn't know what was going to happen when their hands and feet were tied and they were tossed into the flames.

*Shadrach, Meshach, and Abed-Nego answered and said to the*

*king, "O Nebuchadnezzar, we have no need to answer you in this matter. If that is the case, our God whom we serve is able to deliver us from the burning fiery furnace, and He will deliver us from your hand, O king. But if not, let it be known to you, O king, that we do not serve your gods, nor will we worship the gold image which you have set up"* (Daniel 3:16-18).

This is such a beautiful picture of God's deliverance of His children! They were aware of what God was willing to do for them, and they sure did experience a rescue! Not only did God bring them out of the fire unharmed, He caused their enemies to be consumed.

*"...because the king's command was urgent, and the furnace exceedingly hot, the flame of the fire killed those men who took up Shadrach, Meshach, and Abed-Nego"* (Daniel 3:22).

The same God who rescued the Hebrew boys is the God who rescues us. Let the redeemed of the Lord say so! Every time you are thankful or speaking the blessings made available as part of your salvation, you are saying so!

The thing to remember about God is this: if we are ever in a tough situation, we don't have to fear because rescue is available. When we follow God, sometimes things can get challenging. That's what happened to Shadrach, Meshach, and Abednego. And look at Daniel; he served God with his whole heart, but he still was thrown into the lions' den. This is why it says "when," not "if" you go through the fire or the water, you won't be harmed (see Isaiah 43:1-2). We will face certain challenges in life. We must keep our hearts and our mouths full of thanksgiving, declaring the truth in the face of difficult times. In these times, it's vital to declare the promises of God. Speak your promises to your problems!

Keep speaking your sozo rights of rescue, protection, deliverance, safety and security. They are all part of our new birthright. Jesus has paid for us, fully! Countless times, God brought provision to those who needed a "right-now" miracle or His divine intervention. If He did it for them, He has done it and will do it for you. He is the same Deliverer. His promises have not changed. He hasn't changed His mind. Through Christ we have been given all the hope, all the healing, and all the deliverance we will ever need! He has given it, sealed it, and guaranteed it.

*For the Son of God, Jesus Christ, who was preached among you by us—by me, Silvanus, and Timothy—was not Yes and No, but in Him was Yes. or all the promises of God in Him are Yes, and in Him Amen, to the glory of God through us. Now He who establishes us with you in Christ and has anointed us is God, who also has sealed us and given us the Spirit in our hearts as a guarantee* (2 Corinthians 1:19-22).

Rise up and don't allow the enemy or spiritual attacks in this life to get you down! Start right now blessing the Lord, with your hands lifted and your mouth declaring thanks, and as the redeemed of the Lord, keep saying so and you will see the goodness of God!

## ENDNOTES

1. James Strong, The New Strong's Exhaustive Concordance of the Bible (Nashville, TN:  Thomas Nelson, 1991), Hebrew #18.

## CHAPTER FIVE

### Come to the Table

You and I have been chosen by the King of kings, the Father of Glory, the Lord of all creation! We haven't been chosen as servants; we've been adopted into His family! We are His very own children, who cry out in our hearts, *"Abba, Father!"* (see Galatians 4:6). There are infinite benefits for the members of the King's household, and the story of King David's kindness to Mephibosheth is a wonderful portrayal of our invitation to the Lord's table, where our full sozo rights are spread before us!

*Jonathan, the son of Saul, had a son who was crippled in his feet. He was five years old when the news about Saul and Jonathan came from Jezreel, and his nurse took him up and fled, and as she fled in her haste, he fell and became lame. And his name was Mephibosheth* (2 Samuel 4:4).

Through no fault of his own, Jonathan's son Mephibosheth had a disability. His nurse had accidentally dropped him when he was five years old, and from that point on, Scripture tells us that he was lame in both feet. I'm guessing he had some anger and maybe even some resentment over that situation. Anger seems like a probable response, right? From many angles, it looks like life dealt him a bad hand.

As he grew older, we are told that he lived in a place called Lo-debar. *Lo-debar* literally means "no thing", or "not a pasture."[1] Mephibosheth was living in a place essentially called *Nothing*, and he even saw himself through that lens of "nothing," calling himself "a dead dog." Isn't this just like the enemy of our souls? We've all had things happen that weren't our fault. The enemy throws things like trauma, disease, poverty, and a host of other things our way. He loves to poison us with bitterness until we check out and go into hiding, and he convinces us that we have no worth. There we sit, basically immovable, and no amount of self-effort seems to change our circumstances or our perspectives.

*The king said, "Is there not yet anyone of the house of Saul to whom I may show the kindness of God?" And Ziba said to the king, "There is still a son of Jonathan who is crippled in both feet."*

*So the king said to him, "Where is he?" And Ziba said to the king, "Behold, he is in the house of Machir the son of Ammiel in Lo-debar." Then King David sent and brought him from the house of Machir the son of Ammiel, from Lo-debar. Mephibosheth, the son of Jonathan the son of Saul, came to David and fell on his face and prostrated himself. And David said, "Mephibosheth." And he said, "Here is your servant!" David said to him, "Do not fear, for I will surely show kindness to you for the sake of your father Jonathan, and will restore to you all the land of your grandfather Saul; and you shall eat at my table regularly." Again he prostrated himself and said, "What is your servant, that you should regard a dead dog like me?"* (2 Samuel 9:4-8).

## Invited to the King's Table

Mephibosheth was not invited into David's house because of anything he could do for David. He was invited on the basis of the relationship David had with Jonathan. In the same way, the Lord does not invite us to come based on anything we can do, but on what Jesus already did for us. We are invited on the basis of relationship. We are no longer slaves, we are not "dead dogs," as Mephibosheth felt he was; we are sons and daughters through Jesus' shed blood!

David vividly displays the Father's heart when he searches for someone in Jonathan's house to show kindness to, someone he could invite to live in his house and eat at his table. What was the result? A lame man who lived in Nothing became royalty, with all the privileges of the king's household given to him. It's a beautiful picture of what is true for us: God has provided us full rights and benefits as His sons and daughters; we are invited into His house, and we each have a seat at His table with our name on it!

David essentially told Mephibosheth, "everything I have is yours." This is what sonship looks like! The Lord has already provided us with *all* the benefits of sonship, and they're infinitely greater than anything David gave Mephibosheth. The story of their relationship displays what God the Father provides for us, but I tell you, it barely scratches the surface of our blessings! Scripture tells us that we are *"blessed with every spiritual blessing in the heavenly places in Christ"* (Ephesians 1:3).

Imagine how Mephibosheth must have felt when he heard the king was asking for him, a man who couldn't walk, and who likely felt destined to a life of "nothing." Surely it was "exceedingly abundantly more" than he had asked or imagined (see Eph. 3). This is our sozo rights package at work: so much more than we've asked or imagined! Realize this: it's *not* too good to be true! The Lord's promises are not empty. They are all yes and amen in Christ, and they are *for us*. He is *for us*!!

We all have things in our lives that feel like hindrances, and our response to them can be to trust God despite what we see, or to make our home in a place called Nothing. For too long, many Christians have moved into lands of Nothing. We've looked at our painful circumstances and have given in to some form of paralysis where we've stopped walking forward with the Lord. I'm not denying the pain of life's circumstances; we can live through some horrendous experiences. But King David had a plan to get Mephibosheth out of his land called Nothing, and our King has a plan for us, too!

Before Mephibosheth arrived, there was a seat reserved for him at David's table, because the invitation had come from David's heart. The king himself had extended the invitation, so everything Mephibosheth needed was already prepared and waiting for him.

He could have said no. He could have turned down the invitation, and continued with life as usual, a lame man. Though he called himself "a dead dog," he made a decision to accept the king's invitation. David reassured him: *"Do not fear, for I will show you kindness for the sake of your father Jonathan, and I will restore to you all the land of Saul your father, and you shall eat at my table always"* (2 Samuel 9:7).

We've received an invitation from the King of all kings in the same way Mephibosheth was invited by King David! Do we know what we've been offered? Do we know where we've been invited? Our King delights in showing us kindness; He loves to restore; and He is fully committed to us, *always*!

## Sitting Down

The next thing we know, Mephibosheth is seated at the king's table and given joint-heir rights, the full rights of a son; his sozo rights package! *"...So Mephibosheth ate at David's table as one of the king's sons"* (2 Samuel 9:11).

In the same way, you and I have been made kings and priests, or joint heirs, with Jesus! *To Him who loved us and washed us from our sins in His own blood, and has made us kings and priests to His God and Father* (Revelation 1: 6).

Notice Mephibosheth's position at the table. He is seated at the king's table. He's not walking, or running, or standing. In fact, he wasn't physically able to do any of these things. His position was not a result of anything he accomplished on his own. No amount of his striving could have seated him where the king seated him. The same is true for us. Ephesians 1 tells us that this is our legal position: we are "seated with Him in heavenly places." This is God's work through Christ on our behalf, not our work! So often we think we can "earn" something from God through more praying, more Bible study, or more fasting. The good news is, our seat at the King's table is secured because of what *He has already done*, not because of our feeble efforts. We can no more earn ourselves a seat at the table than Mephibosheth could. In fact, his lameness reveals how utterly helpless we are to save ourselves. But because of Love, we have been invited, and not just as guests! We are not visitors to the King's table; this is where we belong!

Notice too, that Mephibosheth's seated position at the table puts him on a level playing field, so to speak. If you're physically lame and you're seated at the table, your feet are under the table. Your lameness is no longer a focus; the focus is now the spread set before you! It's time for us to stop looking at our own disabilities or inabilities and focus on what the Lord has provided. As we do, we will fully partake of the things our King, the Lord Jesus, has made available to us.

There is something deeper happening here that I want you to see. Mephibosheth's invitation to the table was an invitation into the Throne Room of the King. When we come to the Throne Room, we are coming to the Table of the King. The table is not waiting to be set, it's *already* been set. There is *already* a table set before us. This is the revelation of Mephibosheth. No matter our story in life, the table is set, and we, through His immeasurable kindness to His sons and daughters, are invited to come and dine with the King!

## You Have a Right to the King's Table!

Psalm 23 gives us another picture of the table the Lord has provided for us. *"You prepare a table for me in the presence of my enemies…"* Even when you are facing enemies of poverty, sickness, doubt, and other things the enemy brings, you can feast at the Lord's table. It has already been prepared for us. Even more, we can sit and dine *in peace*, even in the presence of great opposition. There is protection at the table! Our assurance isn't in the table, or even the food on the table. Our assurance is in the One who's prepared the table, and who has the confidence to sit it down right in the middle of our enemies, so they will know their sure defeat!

When you understand what is fully yours and that you're already seated with the King of kings, things will no longer be the way they've been. It's time for us to be bold in approaching the Lord for what is already ours. I'm not saying we should be disrespectful in any way; please don't hear that. What I'm saying is that we need to come to the table / the Throne with a Hebrews Four mentality: *Let us therefore come boldly to the throne of grace, that we may obtain mercy and find grace to help in time of need* (Hebrews 4:16).

Aligning ourselves to receive the blessings of the Lord is twofold: there are things we can do to position our hearts, but we're also told that if we come boldly, we will receive! Part of that boldness is that we don't necessarily have to ask for grace, mercy, and help. We can do that, of course, but we can also come boldly and simply receive these benefits already provided! Our boldness is in knowing and understanding what is *already ours* through the Blood of Jesus. There is *already* a seat at the table with your name on it! Let us approach the table, the Throne, with full confidence!

As we close, I want to remind you of a powerful weapon at your disposal: holy communion. The Scripture says we can receive holy communion as often as we desire. The bread and the cup are remembrances that we're seated with the King. As we receive communion, we are remembering what Jesus has provided for us; we are eating at His table. Jesus said, *"do this in remembrance of Me"* (Luke 22:19). A life of communing with Him and partaking of holy communion, remembering His table, will bring your sozo rights into manifestation in your life and the lives of others!

## His Resurrection is Our Resurrection

We've looked at the amazing benefits package the Lord has provided for us. We've examined our position as sons and daughters. We've discussed how we enjoy being under the Law of the Spirit of Life, and how important it is for us to declare the truth of the Father's words over us. And finally, we've seen the table set before us, with our seats reserved, prepared from our Father's heart of love. We've been given so much more than our little minds can understand! Though our sozo rights package is so much more than we can ask or imagine, this is what we're created for. Jesus has prepared the way for us to enter into the fullness of everything He is and everything He has as the Son of the Most High.

Do you remember when Jesus first appeared to Mary in the garden after His crucifixion, and she mistook Him for the gardener? Indeed, He was the Gardener, the last Adam, here to restore what the first Adam lost. The first Garden was a place of no sickness, no disease, no poverty, no lack; everything Adam and Eve needed was provided for them before God ever created them!

Jesus told Mary, *"Do not cling to Me, for I have not yet ascended to My Father; but go to My brethren and say to them, 'I am ascending to My Father and your Father, and to My God and your God"* (John 20:17).

Notice how Jesus describes the Lord. "My Father and your Father...My God and your God." He is doing two things here: first, He is expressing our relationship to Him as co-heirs. For the first time, Jesus says His Father is now *our* Father! Wow! This is the result of His crucifixion, His shed blood on our behalf. Second, He is expressing the Father's heart toward us: fatherhood revelation is what we need first, to help us better understand the power of His deity. Again, wow! Jesus is telling us that in order to have the revelation of Him as the God of Power, we must first know Him as Father.

I want to encourage us all to let this be the season where we press in to know Him as our loving, providing Father. Let's do things differently. Where we've walked by sight, let's begin to walk by faith. Where we've lived in a place of nothing, let's receive the King's invitation to His table and receive our healing, deliverance, and blessings package of our new spiritual birthright. Always remember, He has provided our sozo rights blessings as King of kings and Lord of lords, and the table set before us is set by our Father, through and to the Son, Jesus Christ, with handwritten invitations for all who will come. Let us answer as sons and daughters, the wonderful invitation our Heavenly Father has offered and begin to live declaring SOZO POWER!

## ENDNOTES

1. James Strong, The New Strong's Exhaustive Concordance of the Bible (Nashville, TN: Thomas Nelson, 1991), Hebrew #3810.

NOTES:

NOTES:_____

_____
_____
_____
_____
_____
_____
_____
_____
_____
_____
_____
_____
_____
_____
_____
_____
_____
_____
_____
_____
_____
_____
_____
_____
_____
_____
_____
_____
_____
_____
_____
_____

HANK+BRENDA

For more books and resources from
Hank and Brenda Kunneman,
visit us online at HankandBrenda.org

One Voice Ministries
P.O. Box 390460
Omaha, NE 68139
855-777-7907